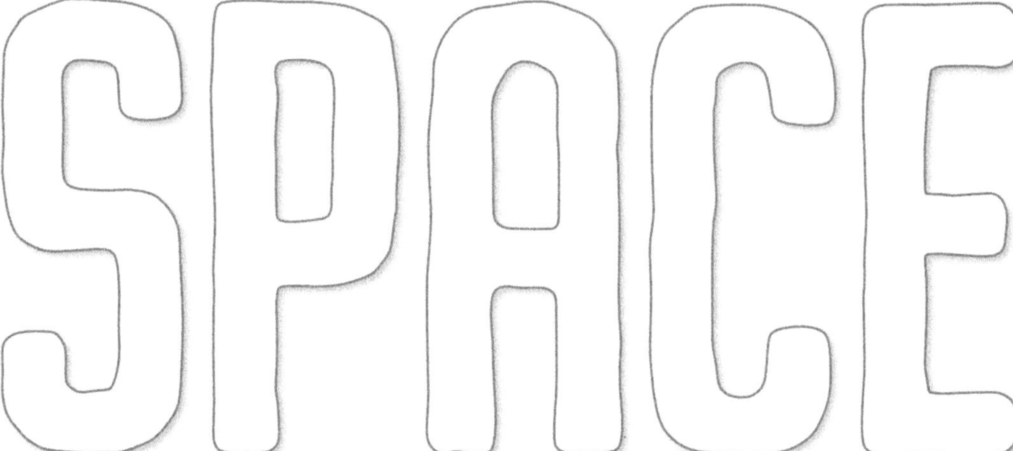

MARLON MONSTER BOOKS

THIS BOOK BELONGS TO

COMMANDER

READY FOR LAUNCH

THE ASTRONAUT WAVES GOODBYE

BLASTOFF

THE ASTRONAUTS ARE ON THEIR WAY

SPACE WALK

EARTH LOOKS SO SMALL FROM UP HERE

LANDING ON THE MOON

DESIGN YOUR OWN FLAG

MY ROCKET

DRAW YOUR OWN ROCKET

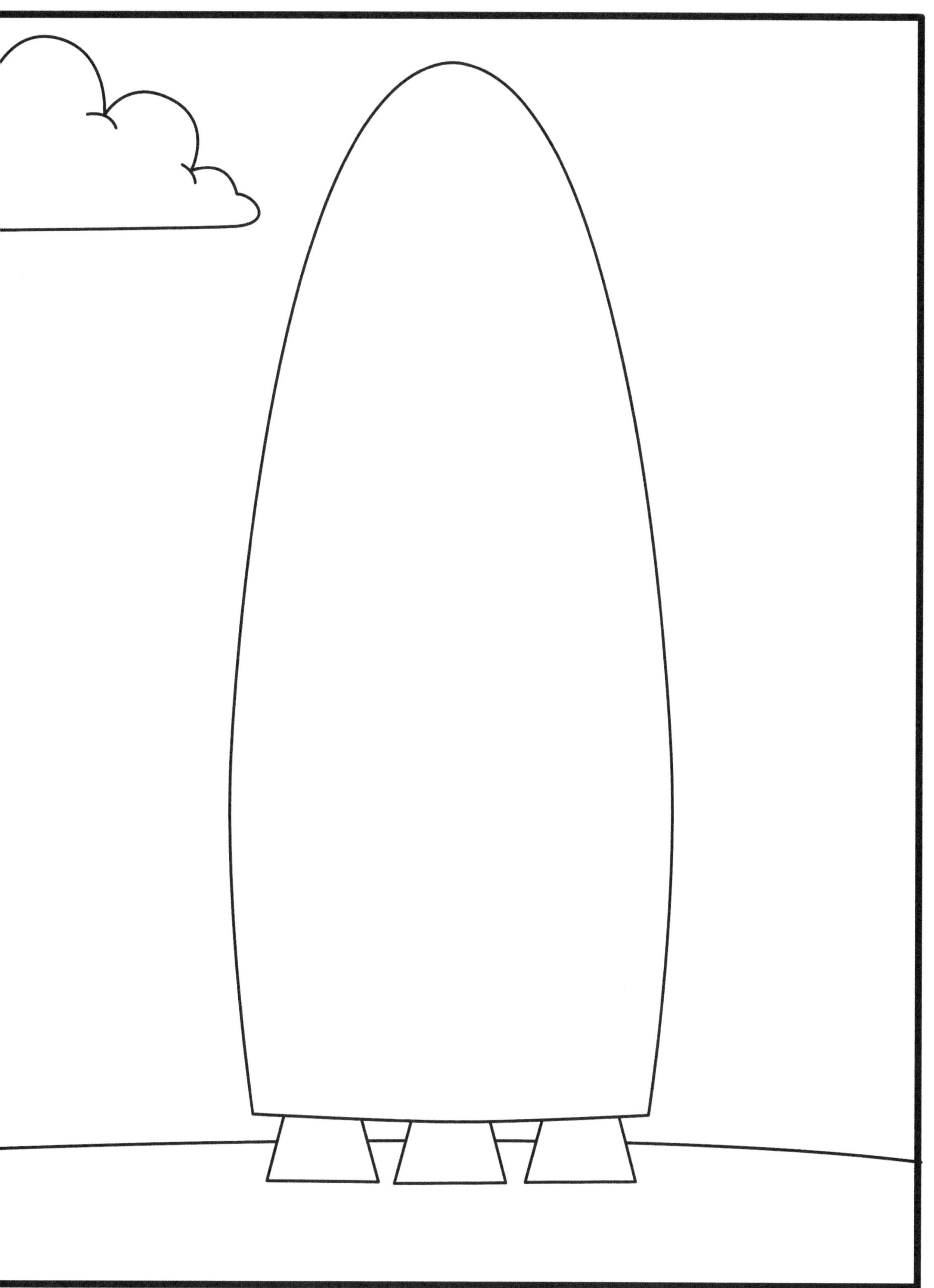

SPACE STATION

THIS IS WHERE THE ASTRONAUTS LIVE

CLOTHES

ASTRONAUTS NEED LOTS OF SPECIAL CLOTHES

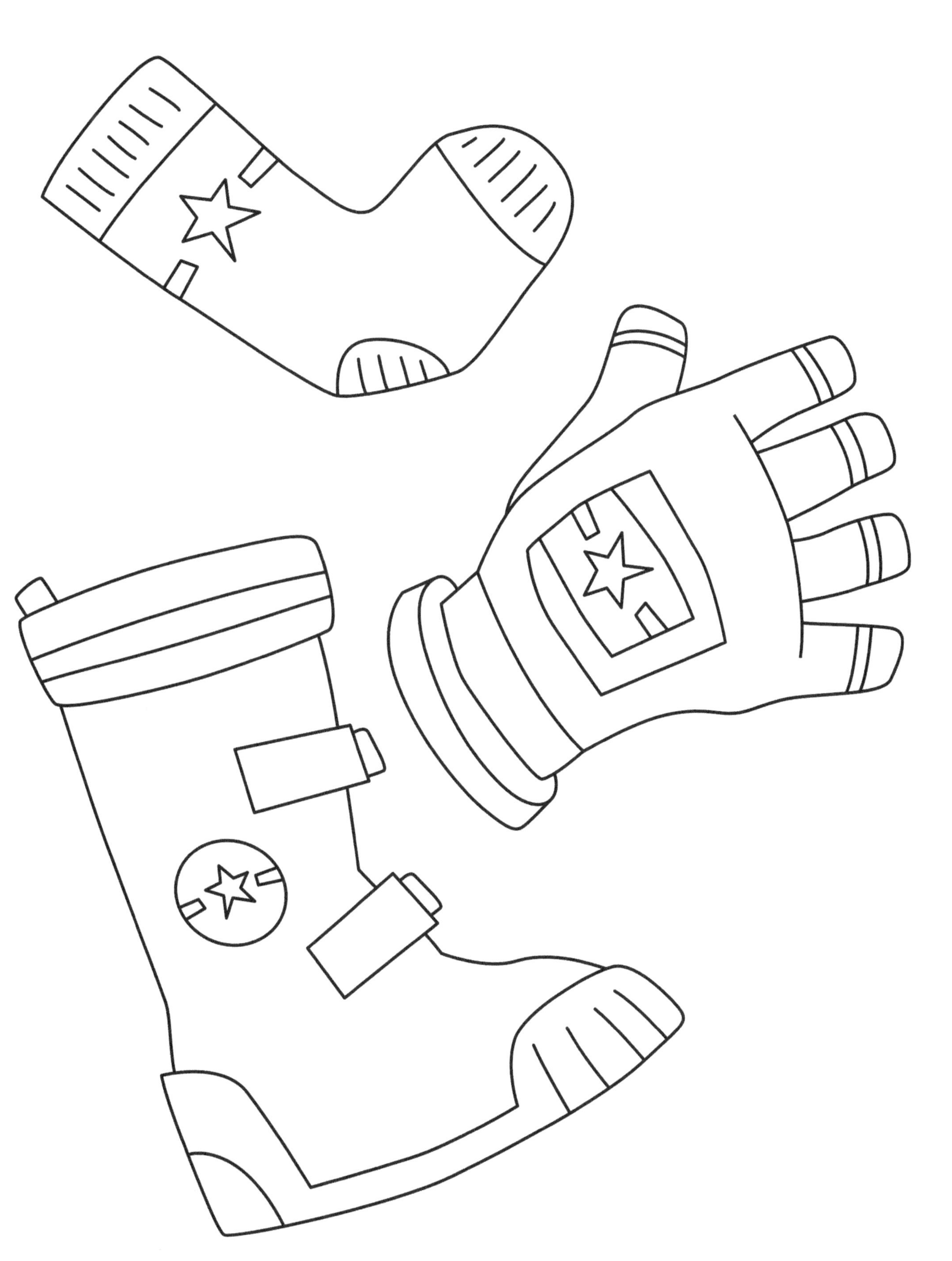

SPACE FOOD

PACKETS OF SPACE FOOD

COOKIES
SPACE
JUICE

EATING IN SPACE IS FUN

IMAGINE YOUR FOOD FLOATING BY

WHAT IS YOUR FAVORITE?

DRAW YOUR FAVORITE FOOD IN THE SPACE PACKET

EXERCISE

YOU HAVE TO KEEP FIT - EVEN IN WHEN THERE IS NO UP OR DOWN

EXPERIMENTS

THESE ASTRONAUTS ARE GROWING PLANTS IN SPACE

FUN

SPACE IS FUN TOO!

SLEEPING IN SPACE

ZZZZZZZ

SATELLITE

SATELLITE HIGH ABOVE THE EARTH

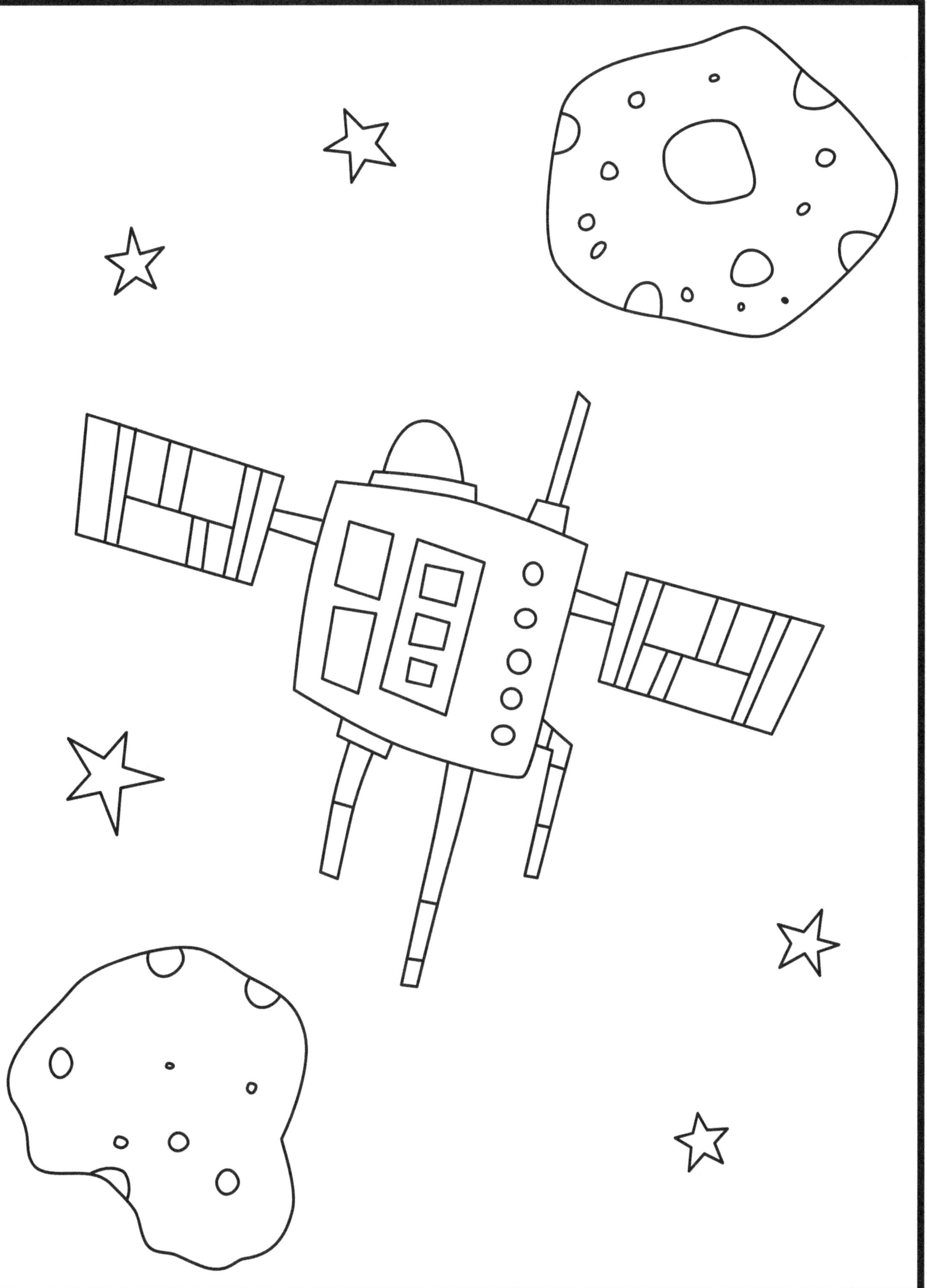

STARS AND PLANETS

OUT IN SPACE

ALIEN SPACESHIPS

LOTS OF DIFFERENT ALIENS

SAY HELLO

IMAGINE MEETING AN ALIEN

ALIENS

I WONDER WHAT THEY LOOK LIKE?

SAY HELLO

WHAT DO YOU THINK THE ALIEN IS SAYING?

SPACE ALIEN

DRAW YOUR OWN ALIEN

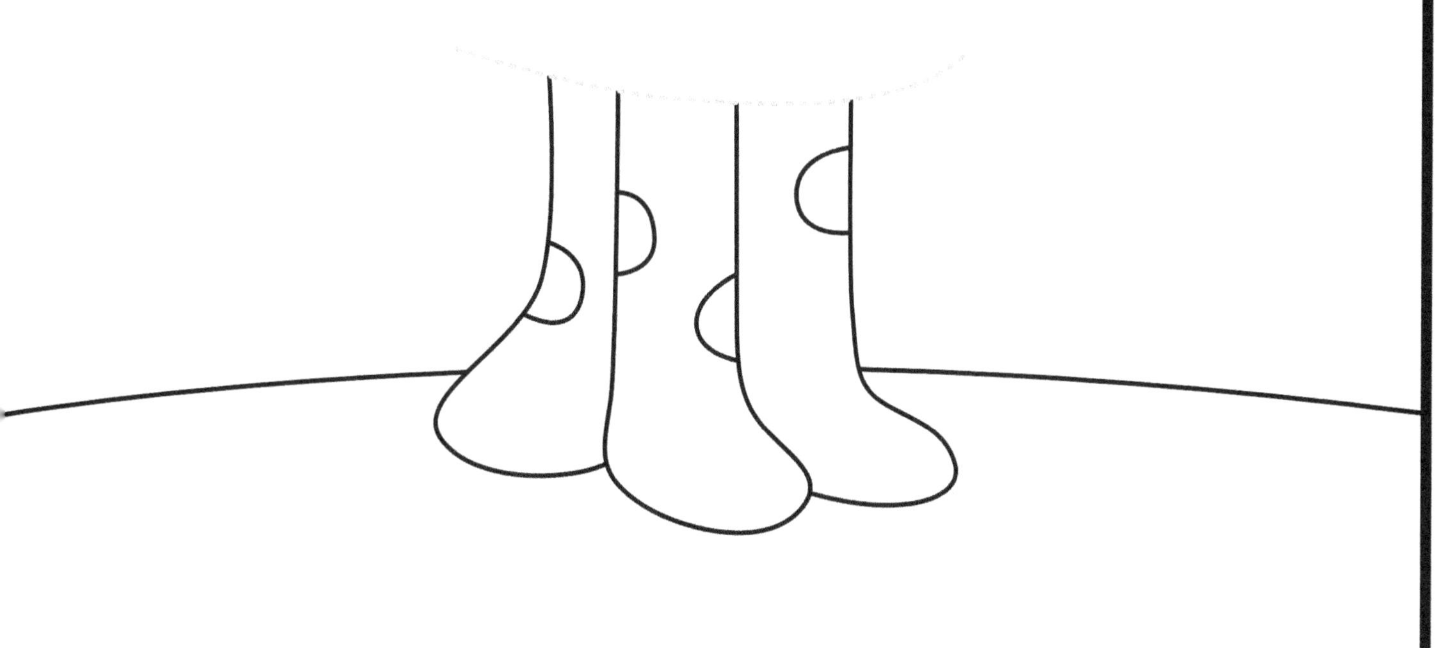

SPACE ROBOT

BEEP BEEP

WOOF

EVEN DOGS HAVE BEEN IN SPACE

SPACE FAMILIES

ONE DAY WE MAY LIVE IN SPACE

TELESCOPE

DON'T FORGET TO LOOK UP AT THE NIGHT SKY

CREATE
A SPACE FOR YOUR OWN CREATIONS

CREATE

A SPACE FOR YOUR OWN CREATIONS

CREATE

A SPACE FOR YOUR OWN CREATIONS

CREATE

CREATE

A SPACE FOR YOUR OWN CREATIONS